American Bitch

American Bitch

Poems by

Rae Hoffman Jager

Karen,
Thank you for the support.

Rae Hoffman Jager

Cover by Shay Culligan
Cover image by Christen Noel Kauffman

ISBN: 978-1-63980-112-1

Kelsay Books
502 South 1040 East, A-119
American Fork, Utah 84003
Kelsaybooks.com

To Ben and Ivy, earthside. To baby Fox Allan and Dad, who should be earthside, but instead are held in these pages.

Acknowledgments

Many thanks to the magazines in which earlier versions of these poems appear: *Writer's Resist, Sports Literate, 2 Bridges, IDK, Midwestern Gothic, Isacoustic, Forklift, Ohio, Orange Blossom Review, SWWIM, Wednesday Night Poetry,* and *Glass, a Journal of Poetry.*

The most heartfelt thanks to poets Sara Moore Wagner, Caroline Davis Plasket, and Christen Noel Kauffman for their endless love, support, and feedback.

Additional thanks to Christen Noel Kauffman for helping create the cover photograph for this book.

Contents

Bull Rush

Hail Mary

Epigraph

The wounded child inside many males is a boy who, when he first spoke his truths, was silenced by paternal sadism, by a patriarchal world that did not want him to claim his true feelings. The wounded child inside many females is a girl who was taught from early childhood that she must become something other than herself, deny her true feelings, in order to attract and please others. When men and women punish each other for truth telling, we reinforce the notion that lies are better. To be loving we willingly hear the other's truth, and most important, we affirm the value of truth telling. Lies may make people feel better, but they do not help them to know love.

—bell hooks, *All About Love: New Visions*

I'm gonna to get mine more than I get got.

—Marshawn Lynch

Running Out the Clock

The practice of preserving a lead by allowing the clock to "run out" without making any risky plays.

The End of the World

It begins with a splinter of some kind,
a bunch of old men sitting in a circle
deciding which laws to bend first.
It sounds like crunching, a wood chipper eating itself.
Outside it always looks like it's going to rain
and that rain is going to burn.
If only you could've seen this coming,
   taken matters into your own hands.
You tried, I remember—climbed a secluded mountain to pray,
hit your phone with a rock, put crystals all over your body,
   and when that didn't work, you gave up.
I am sorry for all those I have failed.
The trees are limp and the old gods dead.
There is no punishment for people
unloading guns into one another.
No turning back, just turning from.

Multiplication

When you first came to me, palms up,
years of other women were hanging from you
like kudzu. We walked together this way
for a long while until one day, you shook them free.
You were born right there before my eyes
and love gave you language. You tested
those first words, pressed them into my mouth—
said, *I am my beloved, and my beloved is mine.*
In return I said, *Here is my body. Eat of my flesh
and drink of my blood.* You touched me with a ring,
and we crawled forward on our hands and knees,
away from the past, sulfuric and blistering with bad news.
There is no past now, only the forgiveness of two
bodies coming together to make something,
anything, if it will grow.

Every Year a Persimmon Reminder

after Li-Young Lee

You must feel a persimmon to know
that its skin is hymen thin.

Gently, my grandmother says,
showing me how to inspect
a body without piercing
through to the syrup and pulp.

I have been this fruit before.
Once captured, once gored,
once oozing. I was 18
on a moonless night
next to a persimmon tree.

I tell no one my story.
How do you explain
that one puncture is all it takes
to make a vacuum?

That much I remember,
the world crawling in.

Every November they arrive
at my grandmother's in a box
from California—each heavy sun
wrapped in paper, fragments
of their wooden umbilical
cords still attached.

She holds those ripe bodies
in her hands, recites a prayer,
and then lets them go.

Sowing

Roots from the spider
plant cuttings drop
and with water,
fatten, grow.

When the time
is right, I place
each small head
in new soil

—recite,
Forgive me, Mother,
for being so unlike

the spider plant
that is merciful,
resilient

—making home
of anything.

I do this for days,
farming. Stopping
only to pray,

until all the roots
have firmly settled,
leaves gone opaque.

Inside, my uterus
drops its heavy
wine—uninhabitable,

acrid, something there
looking for soil,
finding only rocks.

Wreak

after David Wallace-Wells[1]

While we slept, awoke, and made oatmeal,
went to work, walked the dog, and so on,
A crack in the ice shelf grew 11 miles—
raced the ocean where it dropped
with a titanic splash no one heard.

As we make messes, more icebergs calve far off—
tons of carbon released and along with it
pre-historic bacteria and bugs with tentacles
and tusks two feet long.

Even the Doomsday seed vault isn't safe.
Just years after being built on Svalbard,
it flooded. Those small hearts were salvaged,
but that's not the point—every day

we arm the planet with hotter,
dirtier breath to gag us with.

Is your ulcer heating up yet? —

Bangladesh won't last the century. Soon,
Mecca will be pan-fried and Haj, a death march.

I guess there is some irony in that we are a lot like ice,
though there is less and less of it to be found: cold,
full of dangerous gas, and indignantly indentured.

---

[1] A found poem with words from the David Wallace-Wells New York Mag article, The Uninhabitable Earth, that got the Internet defensive and feeling existential dread.

Not all the prayers in the world will rehydrate
the kidneys of the El Salvadorian sugar cane fields,
the wilted grains of the west, and dried-up river beds—

Just wait.

Ode to Data Mining

Call me by my secret name, Google, the one I utter only on G-chat.
Order my boy shorts, size medium, made of cotton and lace.
Suggest my favorite post-rock driving music, Thai food within 5
miles of home. Tell me how to get to work when the arteries of
highway clog, seize. Sell my shower musings. Advertise my small
batch Cumquat-Jalapeno jam to the right demographic. Ok Google,
find.[2] Determine the gender of my future baby. Predict the day I
will die. Tell me what Harry Potter House I am, Goddamnit, and do
it quickly. I don't have much time. Send me videos of hamsters
eating tiny gourmet meals, so I can feel hunger. Load all the
pictures I don't want to see from my relationship back in 2013.
Map my house, Roomba. Sell the floor plans and spoils of wood
floors—all those tiny black dog hairs must be good for something,
something.

---

[2] When reading this poem aloud, the line "Ok Google, find" will most certainly
send your, the reader's, android phone into a tailspin for the meaning of
something.

Straw Millennial

First get a couple degrees in something useful like English or Art History, so you can spend time contextualizing the quotes on limited edition Starbucks cups or identifying the style of old city buildings.

Work as an adjunct and barista, so you can feel the crippling sense of academic stagnancy and worthlessness but get enough coffee to grade on weekends.

Get broken up with by your college boyfriend and a few others because you weren't enough of something they saw on TV.

Obsessively look at houses on Zillow during that time and save up a miraculous 10k by cutting out avocado toast.

Speculate about retirement but only for a minute or two, because even though you saved most of your money, you didn't save enough. Plus, every old white guy who has ever explained to you how investing works smells like rust. You don't trust rust.

So give up on having a more rigid life plan. Throw down 10% of your paycheck on a tab at Ye Ole Taverne and cry a little into your gin and tonics. Have the bright idea to take your dad's camper from 1972 that he tried to get you to live in in grad school.

Start spending your weekends in junkyards learning the songs of old car hoods and refrigerators. Visit garage and yard sales to find the missing pieces you think you need.

Let each nail and screw build you until one day a beautiful house on wheels, that you never planned, is done. Don't live in it. Sell it to one of your students for $30,000. Still spend 10% of your paycheck at Ye Ole Taverne. Admit you don't learn lessons easily.

Build a few more cheap homes and each time feel a little lighter, like all those controlling affluent men hanging off of you—the ones who run city council, university departments, your bank, even the micro governments inside your body, are losing their grip so that something else may grow.

Admit you are good at using your hands, even though grandma says you lack ambition. Laugh because you know most wouldn't even know how to nail together a coffin and yours has wheels.

Fumble Recovery

When the ball is dropped by the offensive team and recovered by either side—in this case, the losing side.

Positive

Because I had visited all the cities I wanted,
drank the coffee and beer with notes of melon,
green apple, and past trauma.

Because I had eaten the oysters and microgreens,
and they were just okay.

Because the drive home always felt empty,
and people always asked when.

Because I could take you into me
and become a house.

I wanted to become a house, a house.

But instead, I became a bucket
and spade

and sat outside with my knees
in the dirt, palms up.

All summer it did not rain.
All winter it did not snow.

All spring it did not
until one day,
I felt something inside me quake.

This could be it, I thought,
and then a cloud broke,
and the rain came down.

More or Less

As the pollution trimester
builds its knives
and pulleys in my gut.

Even the sunsets
are as sick as I am,

      the trees.

And they tell me,
the women who
buzz around my center,

to love it, my job
to carry, empty—

and to be guilty
when I cannot.

And they tell me, too,
it will get easier,

when I know very well
they mean it's all
Stockholm syndrome
from here.

Creation

The man with no lower legs
removes each
prosthetic limb,
unrolls cloth until his knees
are bare. He rubs
the raw caps
in circular motions
the way our plane feels
like it revolves
around the earth.
Knowing some questions
re-wound, I keep my mouth
shut. Instead I massage, too,
my growing belly
as we prepare
for a rough landing.
We do not look
at each other much:
He sips a screwdriver.
I read a book,
both of us children
recovering from that same
first explosion
in the belly
of dying stars.

First Lesson in Violence

There are occasions when I say, pull yourself together, bitch. It could be worse. You could be living in Ancient Greece when women had to turn into laurel trees to avoid getting raped by Apollo, and even then it was no guarantee.

Even if you weren't a woman, I say again to myself, this time in a mirror. Just look at poor Prometheus, oozing from the gut for an eternity on a cliffside, proving that if you could get punished for gifting the world fire, you should worry about breathing too loudly through the nose while eating a sandwich.

If the Greeks dipped their toes into blood, the Romans were the true harbingers of hurt, leaving a trail of perverted emperors and murder through the dark ages up until today—It has never really been a good time for us humans, has it?—which is why I have lied to every man I've ever loved— told them I come from better stock than this

redneck blood grandpa who beat the hell out of his wife and shot her lover in the chest—pretend that when the beginning of time happened, the firstborn wasn't a man, and he didn't nurse so hard he tore the breast from his mother's bone. Because that's what the myth would say, that we still have her blood in our mouth.

The Origin of Football

after RadioLab's Football episode

Organized football was first
created to keep men frontier-hard.
Imagine all of those Ivy Leaguers
in their loafers, emerging from
the libraries to flex their muscles
under the corn sun—the Carlisle
Indian boys newly assimilated
in their oiled hair and ironed slacks,
doing the same. Daddy Roosevelt approved,
and America blushed. For a while
it worked—the game was just a game
until it killed nineteen boys in 1905.
Then Daddy Roosevelt disapproved
because he had a son or some shit.
That was the first time the game changed,
only then it was no longer a game
but an idea that had its hooks deep in the psyche
and flesh of us. Who am I kidding, all football
did was change since the beginning.
Or no, football is change. I don't actually
know what football is. Maybe it's a ball
in motion, hanging in the air with no hands
on it, a note once it has left the mouth
of the trumpet, miners crawling to or from
the opening of a cave, neither in nor out,
but carried.

Rothko's Almost Black as Pregnancy

Spent most of my days
     in hunger in
remember

     how boss reached
into my waste basket
each afternoon
to monitor what I ate—

his eyeballs two crows
flying in place.

Grew so hard then
     on his mud,
and quickly.

My own edges blurring
into comment.

History is Made by the Viktors

When the wars have halted and the smoke clears, the last man standing is always some noodle you'd never expect to survive a fart, Viktor—cowardly, greedy Viktor. Every Viktor I've ever known has been an ass. Viktor eating the last slice of pie. Viktor taking 50 dollars from his grandmother's purse. Caligula Viktor, spoiling the last episode for everyone on social media, Viktor with his hen feather comb-over, Viktor pressing his grubby thumb into all of the peaches in the produce aisle because he is feeling rotten, Viktor buying twelve Bud Lights, not tipping the bartender, and hitting on your wife. Viktors conveniently installed at every atrophied corner of history with a smirk. Because Luck is the true ruler and Viktor has plenty of it. Because Justice is only the name of a tween apparel store. Because it's not the remarkably smart or strong ones that make it out alive, never. Think of all the noteworthy people who fall quietly off the cosmic cliff every year. As my father, whose name is not Viktor, always said—you don't win a chapter in The Book by sticking out your neck. You win by grabbing the nearest blunt object and swinging it around.

Dear Daughter, Tattoos

Because I want to give the mortician something to laugh at.
Because we're so serious all the time.
Because there was nothing better to do.
Because my friend had a needle and a bottle of India ink.
Because the body is not final.
Because my mother told me no.
Because there are some things you don't want to let go.
Because the only way to remember a mantra is to put it on a rib
          or thigh.
Because I had money I didn't need.
Because I had bare skin I didn't like.
Because all my friends were doing it and are still doing it
          and will never stop doing it.
Because my ancestors were tagged against their will.
Because if there's anything I can take back, it's not history.
Because if there's anything I can change, it's myself.
Because If I can celebrate anything, I will.

The Sad Song of Radium Girls

It began with a watch face,
the glowing numbers
that sent America into a frenzy,

working to death to make everything
chemically bright—drinking water,
underwear, toothpaste

but mostly watches
to see time stare back

at night when the pain throbbed
worse, grew, each small crack
radiating along the jaw—there
the radium did its damage.

All those cursed hosts licking
their paint brushes stiff
by day in drafty factories.

Between each stroke,
the era of disinformation thrived—
of smoking and asbestos don't kill,

of the paint isn't to blame, America,
it's just that women can't stop
contracting syphilis.

The urge men have to smear
rather than heal
didn't have to hold the brush.

And how many hands on the wrong side
of history wouldn't give anything
to dig, bore through the smooth
jaws of terrible men instead,

deep enough to draw out
from poisoned pallets,
that vibrant red.

Almost Going Blind with Jun Kaneko

I stared at what I thought was the moon for thirteen whole seconds.
When it burned through fog and cloud above the road,
I thought *Oh shit* and was already blind. For three days I couldn't
see. While confined to my house, I made several large pieces of
art—a giant wooden egg from Dogwood & Spruce twigs
I found crawling around on my hands and knees,
a book with no pages made from the skin of lizards
my cat hunted to feed me, and a new pair of papier-mâché eyes
I stood in front of the mirror holding. Nothing.
I felt some despair but all around me people still had
errands to run, babies to push out, jobs to complain about.
When I thought I could take no more, I turned on PBS for therapy,
listened to a man's voice describe the large and hollow dangos
and neon opera sets of Jun Kaneko.
Though I couldn't see them, I thought—*Damn,* that sounds
like the kind of work that involves physics, a lot of planning,
and above all, time—Nothing that I have. I sat for a while
in self-pity and darkness, shredded up one of my eyes and started
to come to terms with maybe never seeing again.
Then the narrator came to the end of the program with:
"Kaneko doesn't like to explain his work, and if anyone does,
he probably won't agree." I thought to myself, *stop right there.*
Only a male artist could get away with saying something so
ridiculous, and I wracked my brain for all the male
artists, musicians, writers, and athletes that slid through history
comfortably and effortlessly on one-hundred-dollar bills.
That's when my vision returned, slowly in waves of red fire,
and I saw the dangos on the screen before me in their celebrated
mediocrity, some polka dotted, others dripping with long lines of
glaze—certainly a feat of physics and strength but also just two big
balls where the inside had been replaced by a darkness
that occupies so much space nothing else can.

Torture or Preparation

Thank you, George W. Bush and time for giving us
the disparaging right to get Agamemnon mad and burn the
American flag but not kneel for the National Anthem.
It's within this duality that I've been testing my patience
in the strangest way to prepare for birth (and death).
Last week I loaded toys that nag when their wheels turn
into the back of my car, so they could move freely around.
I carried their battery-operated voices with me everywhere I went,
triggering on every turn, brake. I wanted to see how strong I was,
how long I could live with being chipped away from every angle
until eventually no sound on loop nor the people
who make such torture devices could bother me.
And so then I'll turn to my knees, rack those bone white caps with
roses and barbed wire next to feel a quieter pain.
That's what motherhood requires, reaching
for each new and different pain and after that, who knows.

American Baby

Can you sense me in there,
heaving in the hallway,
pausing on the staircase
to exhale this new invisible
labor, head bent to pray?
Dear god of fetal bloom,
same god that made
titans and ivy leaguers,
slave masters and school shooters,
please not this one too.
A bit longer now you'll wait,
as long as it takes to build
a shield the strength of bone
and cartilage. Little heart
of my own brick and mortar,
not all the hope in this world,
choice, nor guarantee.

Baby, Here is a City

When I finally cradle you like a football—
protective and eager, I will say the world
wasn't always like this, child—split
like a rotten walnut, pungent and leaking.
Once everything was green and quiet,
and we didn't know we were naked.
For now, while you are another
hungry organ inside of me, I give you
a tour of this city. You'll one day learn, too,
how to love and fight for something broken.
There on the corner, a boarded-up school,
across from that a convenience shop
with the LED lights around the windows
and bullet proof glass. Just a mile
in either direction, small factories
people pour from as soon as it is dark
and sometimes gunfire. And there, child—
where your great grandpa used to live
when he wasn't at the JCC or theater
or playing tennis with shirtless men he so badly
wanted to love but would dare not, there
in that broken down apartment, like the others
we pass, mold and ivy growing up the sides,
not letting go.

Football Poem

If a football fell from the heavens, would you dance around where it landed? Erect a glass house for its tanned body to be examined? Probably not. But if the Packers or Seahawks are playing on any given Sunday all bets are off. You don the good luck hat and gloves, take a humbling munch of the turf to become one with the field, and pray for a miracle until it hurts. Outside of the stadium, it is no different; you make the lucky crockpot of white chili, drink only Schlitz and Pepsi, and invite over people who respect that same holiness. The dog is afraid to bark. The baby won't cry. The snow waits to fall. In no other part of life do we defy all logic quite in this way (with a few exceptions, like the snake-handling Pentecostals, which we won't get into for the sake of this poem). Why is that? Does no one talk about how players punt and tackle despite your devotion? Score and break despite your ritual? Guess not. I'm sorry if you were expecting something grand here. You shouldn't have. I mean, this poem could've really become something, but I'm a little distracted by this game—2 minutes left, Packers have the ball, down six with no timeouts.

House by Any Other Name

There is a name for the way I look at you
when I am angry and give up on indulging
in conversation, a different name for each
June night—one with rain, another with fireflies,
one without moon. There are many names
for snow I'll never hear, men I'll never love,
foods I don't cook well. I had many names
given to me after birth—one English,
one Hebrew, one animal, one when mom called
me from the back porch to leave the creek bed
and come home for spaghetti bake. A name for wood
when it bows, weathers, which is different for metal
when it does the same. There is a kingdom,
a class, a genus for living organisms we use.
How we love to make sense of what we have to live with,
a name for the final desperate look my mother
gave her house before handing over the keys to a stranger—
I want to talk about house, just one name
for anything that accommodates something else.
It's complicated having so many words.
Right now, I am a house for my daughter,
a mass of cells I cannot name, whose name
I have not found yet, and that I live in.

Rothko's Almost Black as Childhood

Spent most of my days
in parentheses,

      in black, how it shifts
under different light.
How some days it doesn't.

I looked so closely
at my life then
I looked away.

It's terribly
hard to arrive

      turning back,

what it felt like then to be
consumed young anything.

Train Nigun[3]

Do you remember, sis, how afraid
I was when the trains braked
behind our house late at night—
engines screaming like a girl dragged
by her hair down the lightless track?
I'd sustain a loud hum over that noise,
while I rocked myself back to sleep or tried—
a sound to keep me company for as long
as my lungs could hold air or until dad
appeared in the doorway,
his hands black with car guts.
Sometimes you'd be awake to witness
his face in the smudged dark, his voice
as he yelled at me to shut the hell up,
and my prayer—muted by the suburban
song of un-rescue.

---

[3] A Nigun is a melody or tune hummed or sang as a prayer of joy or lament.

Still Life of Repo Without a Tow Truck

Every once and a while my father
would put down his wrench
and begin his repo ritual—puff out
his chest, smooth his mustache,
open the top drawer of his desk,
and touch the handle of his gun.
He'd send for all six of us to come along.
My mother bristled in the front seat
of the van as she dropped him off in
front of a garage he'd have to pull open—
anything on the other side. It's dangerous
but less so with cute kids, so we'd peer
out the smudged tinted glass
with our big brown eyes, like dad asked,
as some ran from their houses to threaten
or curse us. We couldn't hear
over the sound of idling van,
but occasionally we saw through the
windows of those houses, a child our age,
equally prisoner staring back, neither
one of us daring to look away.

Bull Rush

A forceful and bull-like rush a defensive player makes towards an offensive player to establish control.

Spite as an American Value

Jewish blessings for various occasions
are as numerous as patron saints.
There is a blessing for smelling sweet wood,
taking new clothing, seeing a philosopher,
coming upon the place where one has endured
life threatening danger, and running into
a friend after a year of their absence,
but no blessing for a minority of any kind
moving to a small town in Northern Kentucky.

Likewise, there's a patron saint
for charcoal burners, beekeepers,
and hangovers, but no one to watch over
the exiled. I turn over the leather-bound
prayer book my grandfather gave me—
the one he carried through
each Kentucky town his family was driven from.

It's hard not to hold onto his anger,
but even harder to hold onto his god,
which I abandon as simply as some
their last names like I.W. Harper,
last name actually Bernheim.
As an immigrant, he would've never
been trusted to distill bourbon,
but with a borrowed heritage, he did just that—
coddled the secret to survival that one
can't learn unless they've first
known pursuit:

the half assimilation, half preservation,
half acceptance with half reprisal, the long con,
the make-them-love-you-before-you-tell-them-
who-you-really-are, the lie that needs no prayer,
no saint but god you want one
to carry you through living amongst
strangers.

Showing up at My Childhood Synagogue for the First Time in Ten Years to Show my Catholic Husband How Jews Celebrate

A wiry man with scotch on his breath
and the remnants of an Old World accent
hands me a Torah dressed in its best
necklace and tunic, and because I can't run
away fast enough and wouldn't survive
a 40-day fast if I drop the scrolls,
I hug that heavy body tight, like I held my love
together when his grandpa died
and his torso shook like it would fall apart,
like the teakettle ready for takeoff every night
and suddenly, there I am to lift it away.
That old drunk bat hands me, an atheist goy fucker
and woman full of witchcraft, the holiest of all Jewish artifacts.
So I dance a bit to the sound of a keyboard pounding away
quarter notes, and my confused husband stands sandwiched
between singing in what might as well be jibberish,
not knowing that what echoes back from the vaulted ceiling
is just a shadow of the rich chord from which it was born.
It fills distant corners of the sanctuary all the way
to a coat closet where my 13-year-old self is hiding—
talking to some folded aluminum chairs, gagging
on nips of scotch stolen from the liquor cabinet,
crippled not by the fear of old hides painted
with powerful words, but the men who die holding them.

American Sabbath

On Friday nights, I didn't go to Cowboy Football games at the high school. Instead, mom loaded the fourteen-passenger van and drove us to Grandma's for Shabbat dinner. I resented lighting those yellow candles, singing in a dead language that separated me from the living. Resented that salty brisket and raisin kugel, getting kisses from old ladies with knuckles the size of golf balls. They smelled already dead. I wanted to paint blue horseshoes on my cheeks and rumble the aluminum bleachers with my fists. I wanted to wear a denim skirt above the knees and get high off the testosterone on the turf. Talk to boys whose last names didn't end in -berger and -stein. Feel hot in the cheeks and fingers and not because of guilt. Bow to some other empty god for a change.

Football is Loneliness

Sometimes it's not the field I see when I blink
at a game on TV but a yellow short grass prairie
with buffalo snorting hot breaths into obscure
low hanging clouds. It's Kansas, chewing ugly
the cud of my memory, reminding me
of the brief time I lived in Wichita.
I hated everything then except the Ulrich Museum of Arts
and the city of Salina, where poetry in the Brownback[4] drought
fled to seek refuge in. I found no solace, only whiskey
when I could afford it. When waking up
every morning felt like leaving. When my pen
became water in my hands. When each day
erased the last. When there was no escape,
and we didn't know we were lonely
because we didn't have anything to weigh
ourselves against but the empty prairie, oppressive
blue sky, all those stadiums we shouted into,
none of which ever echoed back.

---

[4] The former governor of Kansas was infamous for siphoning the arts and womens' rights out of Kansas and being booed at at the 2016 NCAA Shockers Game.

Undeliverance

Not by hand of God, despite what the old scholars say, not by fiery messenger, nor by fashionable angel in fur and pearls. Not by matzo ball soup my grandmother carries in a pot in clumsy steps from the stove top to the table set for twenty, with each sway a stomp, each stomp a sway, broth spilling over the edges. Not by candlelight nor prayer, sorry nor psalm. Not by exodus nor fast because not by body, for Christ's sake, but what the body does— open to the world and all those peculiar smells—ground white fish, horseradish, salt, copper hand washing bowl digging into me its thorns all the days of my life.

Unready

My gowned husband, the silent
receiver waiting to catch the ball
of my labor, the celestial cheese
and slop.

       It won't be long now.
Dr. M reaches her hand inside
to check.
              There, she says,
and an electrical circuit breaks.

I knew this wouldn't be easy,
being broken for love,
but I learned to relinquish
when I was born a woman.

My husband's eyes,
they are stormy and afraid
because there's so little
he has needed to sacrifice.

She could slip through
his fingers, he thinks,
and she might.

Immaculate Reception

Hail Mary, baptize me
in Budweiser or the tears
of a man who doesn't cry at births
or funerals, but is weeping now
as he remembers 1972,
Raiders-Steelers, five seconds to go
when the Steelers' ball carried by chance,
ping pongs its way into Franco Harris's hands.
How holy it is to witness
that brief tenderness—the crowd
pouring over their seats like water.
Fuqua being carried out to sea.
Even to this day, no angle
broken down frame by frame,
can solve the mystery that propels the tale
of one man's miracle
and another man's loss.
How afraid some men are
of their own water.

American Bitch

When the first baby descended,
mothers must've bowed dutifully,
the way a work horse takes to its front knees.

I labored on all fours until blood
and centuries of fear crept in—
in droves how it drenched
through towel and robe.

We raced to the hospital then, daughter,
right when I thought my pelvis
would crack like a tree branch
giving itself away to gravity.

You came into this world fist first.
The space you left filled with 'til death
do us part, with white hot milk.

Open your eyes, you bruised and purpled
fruit. Unfold and taste the first betrayal
of this world.

Namesake

Girl is all you were for 12 hours,
red and covered in down.
I wanted to name you something
infectious and hard to destroy—
how exactly does one name something
they've only known from the inside?
I'm drunk with power but tired.
I fall asleep and wake only to nurse.
No one is here for the mother.
Even the mother is not here for herself.
Lots of babies were born on this day,
had names ready on cakes, envelopes,
families huddled around
breathing their new syllables to life.
I fall asleep I wake I fall asleep,
the baby clings to my breast with her fingertips.
Outside a cardinal nags, busies itself
making a nest of hair, matches, and cigarette butts.
English Ivy works its way up from the parking lot,
through the sidewalk, over the fence,
and up each yellow brick to see the girl
who will take its name.

The Continuation of Football

Some cracking sounds
make room for the roar
that follows—a Bill's fan
going through a frozen table,
the after-roar that picks him up.
Other cracking sounds
are hideous, final—
a spine snapped, skull
shattered. That stillness of prayer,
a boy's body on the grass
and everyone hovering over him—
that same boy in a wheelchair
one month, one year,
then forty-five later—all of those years
during which no one looks
at him the same way or at all.
No one quits putting on
their helmets and pads.
Nevermind that one-
in-a-million boy, that hideous
crack he fell through
and out the other side.
We don't remember that sound—
just enjoy the game.

Concussion Poem

A warm body for the field to eat—
hit run hit run on autopilot all day.
Please no more dance for this titan
at the Percocet ballet.
The zone is a riptide
designed to swallow you whole.
Kid, get back out there,
Daddy's got money to make.
The doctor said it's fine;
the double vision will go away.

Hail Mary

The last desperate attempt a losing team makes to throw the ball long across the field, in the hopes that someone will catch it at the last second and score a miracle touchdown that wins the game.

Postpartum Moon

Who's there to hold me while I hold the baby only the dried apricot
moon deflated moon fallen moon tin can tumbleweed moon each
rib awakening against the road winter solstice moon the black
night never ending with its harmonica moon because the
harmonica is like the mother a lonely thankless instrument my
baby pulls hot ribbons of milk from my breast I shrink at her
mouth I shrink at the dark the clock will not turn the moon is
maybe just a hole in the sky where the past burns through it holds
onto you maybe the moon does not matter the moon definitely
doesn't matter the girl will still be hungry so you empty

CTE[5]

Unholy temples   pressure mounting third time today
I'd drive home and sleep but I can't
remember the way   10,000 hits 50,000 yards
of turf   ringing ears   of black dots   burst stars
          1 billion made 1 billion I'd give back
to hold my daughters name in my mouth few more—
where I'd be   In the zone.
learning the more I live   less I know.
I be damned   remembering
head first   way I came
way I go

---

[5] Chronic Traumatic Encephalopathy is a degenerative brain disease that affects athletes who have experienced repetitive trauma to their heads.

Milk Blues

Chained to the bed and awake at 2am
with my nipples hostage
in the mouth of my new master,
I think about razors in the bathroom,
bleach beneath the kitchen sink,
each wooden stair her small body
could tumble down—
that small body I love and fear,
how it erases some edges
and amplifies others. Turns me
into a crazed milk slave. I am nothing
but the milk, nothing without
the milk. I am awake with my milk,
alone with my milk,
counting all the ways
in which before this
came nothing
and after too.

Confessions of a Fantasy Football Addict

Forgive me, Father, for I've sinned.
I've been counting yards all day.
I've traded running backs I used to love
        for running backs I hate to need.

I've been checking stats on my desktop, tablet, phone.
I've cheered for two teams playing against one another.
I've prayed for the injuries and failure
        of decent men.
I've trash-talked, lied, and summoned the Draft King.
I've put all five leagues before my family.

It's not about the money.
        I'm just a competitive person.
Is it so wrong, Father,
that I get high
playing those unpredictable
bodies for the one day
it will all go
        my way?

Almost Every State Bird, the Cardinal and the
Mother

On this fashionably warm winter day,
a variety of birds overcrowd the dogwood
like a suburban McDonald's lobby.

I watch to see who is wooing who,
count how many fragile talons can fit
on one branch. I measure each
of their calls but cannot discern
any bird other than the cardinal—

ordinary in its flimsy red-brown jacket,
hungry and opinionated,
casting its *cheeseburgerrr, cheeseburgerrr*
order up into the heavens,
and what comes down is more birds.

I stand at the window and admire,
listen to the other shrill bags of air
vibrating the tree
like the holy lung of a monk.
I open the window to get closer.

I step outside, stand under
the nearest branch to listen harder
while inside the baby sleeps
in between discovering that she, too,
has a voice that I do not yet understand.

And when she sends it upwards,
something finds its way down to her,
and it is also ordinary,
vibrating, and holy.

To the Man Who Messaged Me Years ago on a Dating App to Say I'd Probably Die of Breast Cancer Because I was a Jew

At sixteen, I hiked some of the Appalachian Trail.
I climbed 2,000 feet up a running creek in my brother's hiking
boots. I drank from a stream and didn't get sick
even after I found the rotting raccoon carcass at the top of the hill.
I got nine or ten whole miles into the woods,
baptized myself under the name Gingko
before having to turn around and hike out.
My best friend had a bad case of constipation. We all felt blocked.
At twenty, I sang with the Asheville Opera Company—
one young face among thirty—not a huge accomplishment,
but in Angela Brown's shadow, I felt like I could do anything.
So around thirty, I tried—published a very small collection
of poems I never saw royalties to—
married and got pregnant with a girl and hell,
thought that was my peak and maybe it was.
I hope you're writing this down. It's important.
I looked at my blood results and thought of you.
It turns out you were right. Eventually, I'll have to be hollowed out
from tit to taint. You've cut open a cantaloupe before
and removed the seeds and gore. It will be like that.
They'll stitch me up with new slits I'll never be able to see from.
Even then my genes may continue to rot. I am not here
to thank you. I am here to tell you I've done what makes me
happy and then some. I am here to follow you home from work,
hunt you in dark alleys, lay at the back of your mind like a rotting
carcass. Listen closely—I will collect every piece of myself
in a jar the day they cut me open—a pillowcase, garbage bag, or
hot air balloon. I will sew for you a cape of my ducts and tubes.
Pin them to your neck, so you can feel me always at your back.

A Man Tried to Take my Baby at Huddle House in Corbin, KY

Twenty-five vultures circled above the state road that day.
We looked and looked for a carcass but found nothing.
In the backseat, our daughter slept with no idea
that there are creatures in this world that live off of death.

Duty

The catalpa flowers hang open
like rows of baby teeth
mouthing the streets.
My daughter's eyes clear more
everyday. I take her to see
her first parade, memorializing the dead—
their many faces glued to poles,
taped to store windows. Men long dead
until you get closer and see
they are boys. I hold her to me
and say, *listen girl, this country*
was built on the bones
of the willing and unwilling,
the lucky and cursed.
She coos and smiles at the sirens,
the ROTC teenagers in fatigues
with peach fuzz still on their cheeks.
How can I tell her I brought death
into her life, breathed it into her lungs,
that I gave her no choice?
And that must be how it feels
to serve something. Even nature serves.
This round of bloom, the Honeysuckle.
Next, the Catalpa trees.
After that, the Tulip Poplars
standing guard—so pungent,
so temporary, repeat.

End of the World

Around Kentucky, entire cities flood.
In California, neighborhoods burn to the ground.
Everything feels as heavy as Magnolia Blossoms smell.
We meant well, didn't we, when we erected factories,
made a production line of our bodies,
and told robots to pick up the slack?
Here we are staring at kittens again to forget
that our children are malnourished and hiding
guns in the back of their shorts. Summer,
you're almost here to kill us with your waterboard heat.
I will take my daughter into the community pool to splash.
When fear cripples me, we will stay in the house
with the air conditioner on high, watching smog settle
into the city like dirty milk in a bowl. I'll play the guitar.
My daughter will shake a musical egg. She'll suck on it,
bang it against the counter. Eventually it will shatter
on the kitchen floor, seeds of sound spilling everywhere.

About the Author

Rae Hoffman Jager holds a BA from Warren Wilson College and an MFA from Wichita State University. Her poetry has been published in a variety of online and print journals. In 2016 She was named The New Voice Poet out of Salina, Kansas. This book originally was a finalist with Sundress and *Birdcoat Quarterly* before finding a home with Kelsay Books. When Rae is not writing and publishing poetry, she is spending her time as a birth doula and yoga teacher. She lives on a big hill in Bellevue, KY with her living daughter, son in the stars, spouse, and two old dogs.